contents

British & North American Readers
Please note that Australian cup and spoon
measurements are metric. A quick conversion
guide appears on page 63.

straight from the shelf

It's next to impossible to have a pantry that will cater for all recipes and occasions but, if you can stock your kitchen with as many of the following ingredients as possible, you'll be able to create a wide variety of delicious meals from this book.

pantry

anchovy fillets
antipasto vegetables
    (bottled)
bamboo shoots (canned)
barbecue sauce
basil pesto
bay leaves
borlotti beans (canned)
brandy
bread
butter beans (canned)
capers
capsicum, char-grilled
    (bottled)
cardamom, ground
chickpeas (canned)
chillies, chopped (bottled)
coconut milk
cooking-oil spray
coriander, ground
corn chips
corn kernels (canned)
cornflour
couscous
cracked black pepper
creamed corn
cumin, ground

curry paste, mild
curry powder
dates, dried
eggplant, char-grilled
    (bottled)
five-spice powder
flour, plain
garlic, crushed (bottled)
ginger, grated (bottled)
green peppercorns
    (canned)
hoisin sauce
honey
italian dressing
lentils, red
maple syrup
mexican chilli powder
mixed spice
moroccan seasoning
mustard (french, seeded)
noodles (dried egg, dried
    rice, hokkien, instant)
oil (olive, peanut,
    sesame, vegetable)
oregano, dried
oyster sauce

pasta
peanut butter, crunchy
pine nuts
plum sauce
potatoes, small (canned)
red kidney beans (canned)
redcurrant jelly
rice (basmati, long-grain)
saffron threads or powder
sambal oelek
satay sauce
sesame seeds
sherry, dry
soy sauce
spaghetti
stock (beef, chicken,
    vegetable)
sugar (brown,
    caster, white)
sun-dried tomatoes in oil
sun-dried tomatoes,
    dehydrated
sweet chilli sauce
tabasco sauce

taco seasoning
tandoori paste
teriyaki sauce
thyme, dried
tikka curry paste
tomato pasta sauce
tomato paste
tomatoes (canned)
tortillas, flour
tuna (canned)
vinegar (balsamic, red wine, white, white wine)
wine (dry red, dry white)
worcestershire sauce

refrigerator
butter
chicken, cooked
cream
eggs
mayonnaise
milk
mozzarella cheese
olives, black
parmesan cheese
salami
sour cream
tomato sauce
yogurt

freezer
corn kernels
green beans
peas
seafood marinara mix
smoked cod fish steaks
spinach
stir-fry vegetables

vegetables
avocado
basil, fresh
bean sprouts
broccoli
butternut pumpkin
button mushrooms
capsicum (red, yellow)
carrot
celery
chives, fresh
coriander, fresh
corn cobs
flat-leaf parsley, fresh
kumara
lebanese cucumber
leek
lemon

mint, fresh
onion (brown, green, red, white)
orange
potato
rocket
rosemary, fresh
snow peas
spinach
tomatoes
zucchini

meat & fish
beef fillet
beef minute steak
beef rump steak
beef sirloin steak, boneless
blue-eye cutlets
chicken breast fillets
chicken tenderloins
chicken thigh fillets
chicken wings
flathead fillets
lamb cutlets
lamb fillets
lamb loin chops
pork fillet
pork midloin butterfly steaks
veal cutlets
veal medallions
veal steaks
white fish cutlets

snacks from the shelf

1
Carefully split two pitta bread rounds in half horizontally. Lightly brush inside of each round with melted butter, then sprinkle with grated parmesan cheese and a little paprika. Cook bread rounds in microwave oven, one at a time, on a microwave roasting rack, uncovered, on HIGH about 1½ minutes or until crisp. Cool, then break into pieces. Serve with dips.

2
For a quick sweet chilli dip, combine 250g softened cream cheese with ¼ cup sweet chilli sauce and 1 tablespoon chopped fresh coriander.

3
For a quick beetroot dip, blend or process drained canned beetroot with plain yogurt, ground coriander and ground cumin.

4
Spread one side of sheets of ready-rolled puff pastry with pesto; sprinkle with grated parmesan cheese. Cut each pastry sheet in half; cut each half, widthways, into 1cm strips. Twist pastry strips; place on lightly greased oven trays. Bake in hot oven about 10 minutes or until browned and puffed.

5
Combine chopped fresh tomato, grated mozzarella cheese and drained, finely chopped, canned anchovy fillets. Top slices of toasted Italian bread with tomato mixture; grill until cheese melts.

6
Spread pizza base with olive paste, then sprinkle with grated cheddar cheese; bake in moderate oven until cheese melts and base is crisp.

4

7

For Mexican chicken jaffles, place one slice of buttered bread, buttered-side down, into sandwich maker. Top with combined chopped cooked chicken, taco sauce and grated cheddar cheese. Top with one slice of buttered bread, buttered-side up; cook in sandwich maker until browned.

8

To make parmesan crisps, place tablespoons of finely grated parmesan cheese onto baking-paper-lined oven trays, allowing five per tray (biscuits will spread during cooking). Press tops lightly then sprinkle with sesame seeds and freshly ground black pepper. Bake in moderate oven about 12 minutes or until browned and crisp.

9

For quick gourmet pizza, spread a prepared pizza base with tomato pasta sauce, top with drained sun-dried tomatoes, quartered canned artichoke hearts, seeded black olives and grated mozzarella cheese. Bake in very hot oven about 10 minutes or until browned and crisp.

10

For spiced roasted nuts, combine macadamias, raw cashews, blanched almonds and shelled pistachios in baking dish; bake, uncovered, in moderately slow oven about 15 minutes or until nuts are browned lightly, stirring twice during cooking. Add chilli flakes and sea salt, stir until well combined.

spicy beef and vegetables

700g beef rump steak, sliced thinly
¼ teaspoon five-spice powder
⅓ cup (80ml) black bean sauce
⅓ cup (80ml) oyster sauce
1 teaspoon bottled crushed garlic
2 teaspoons bottled chopped red chilli
85g instant noodles
1 tablespoon peanut oil
1 medium brown onion (150g), sliced thinly
375g packet frozen stir-fry vegetables

Combine beef, five-spice, sauces, garlic and chilli in medium bowl.
Cook noodles in medium saucepan of boiling water, uncovered, until just tender; drain.
Heat oil in wok or large frying pan; stir-fry beef mixture and onion, in batches, until beef is browned. Stir-fry vegetables.
Return beef mixture to wok with noodles, tossing to combine ingredients.

serves 4
per serving 17.8g fat; 1893kJ
on the table in 25 minutes

chicken with spicy peanut sauce

700g chicken
  breast fillets,
  chopped coarsely

spicy peanut sauce
1 tablespoon peanut oil
1 small brown onion
  (80g), chopped finely
1 teaspoon curry powder
½ teaspoon sambal oelek
⅓ cup (90g) crunchy
  peanut butter
⅔ cup (160ml)
  chicken stock
½ cup (125ml)
  coconut milk
2 teaspoons brown sugar
2 teaspoons soy sauce

Thread chicken pieces onto eight skewers.
Cook skewers on heated oiled grill plate (or grill
or barbecue) until browned and cooked through.
Serve skewers with spicy peanut sauce,
and steamed rice with chopped coriander
stirred through, if desired.
Spicy peanut sauce Heat oil in medium
saucepan; cook onion, curry powder and
sambal oelek, stirring, until onion is soft.
Stir in peanut butter, stock, coconut milk,
sugar and sauce; bring to a boil. Reduce heat;
simmer, uncovered, until sauce thickens.

serves 4
per serving 32.9g fat; 2095kJ
on the table in 35 minutes

tip Soak bamboo skewers in water for about
an hour before use to prevent them from
splintering and/or scorching.

chicken in red wine and tomato sauce

2 tablespoons olive oil
2 medium white onions
  (300g), sliced thinly
1 teaspoon bottled
  crushed garlic
700g chicken thigh
  fillets, halved
250g button mushrooms,
  sliced thinly
2 x 425g cans tomatoes
½ cup (125ml) chicken stock
¼ cup (70g) tomato paste
¼ cup (60ml) dry red wine
2 teaspoons brown sugar
1 teaspoon cracked
  black pepper
¼ cup coarsely chopped
  fresh basil

Heat oil in large saucepan; cook onion and garlic, stirring, until onion is soft. Remove onion mixture from pan.
Cook chicken, in batches, in same pan until cooked through.
Return onion mixture and chicken to pan; stir in mushrooms, undrained crushed tomatoes, stock, paste, wine, sugar and pepper. Bring to a boil. Reduce heat; simmer, uncovered, until sauce has thickened slightly.
Remove from heat; stir in basil.

serves 4
per serving 22.6g fat; 1810kJ
on the table in 30 minutes

spicy chicken wings

1kg chicken wings
1 tablespoon peanut oil
1 teaspoon bottled
  grated ginger
1 teaspoon bottled
  crushed garlic
2 tablespoons soy sauce
¼ cup (60ml) hoisin sauce
1 tablespoon sweet
  chilli sauce
2 teaspoons caster sugar
½ cup (125ml) water
3 green onions,
  chopped finely

Cut chicken wings into pieces at joints.
Heat oil in wok or large frying pan; stir-fy
ginger and garlic over heat until aromatic.
Add sauces, sugar and the water; stir over
heat 1 minute. Add chicken; cook, covered,
about 15 minutes, stirring occasionally, or until
chicken is cooked through. Stir in onion.
Serve with steamed baby bok choy, if desired.

serves 4
per serving 13.8g fat; 1295kJ
on the table in 35 minutes

mustard and rosemary chicken

⅓ cup (95g) french mustard
¼ cup (70g) seeded mustard
¼ cup (60ml) lemon juice
2 tablespoons olive oil
1 teaspoon bottled
  crushed garlic
1 tablespoon cracked
  black pepper
1 tablespoon coarsely
  chopped fresh rosemary
6 small zucchini (390g),
  halved lengthways
1 small red capsicum
  (150g), sliced thinly
8 chicken thigh fillets
  (800g), halved
1 tablespoon coarsely
  chopped fresh
  flat-leaf parsley

Preheat oven to hot. Combine mustards, juice, oil, garlic, pepper, rosemary, zucchini and capsicum in large bowl; add chicken. Cover; stand 10 minutes.

Remove chicken from marinade; reserve marinade and vegetables. Place chicken on an oiled rack in baking dish; bake, uncovered, in hot oven about 15 minutes or until cooked through.

Meanwhile, place reserved marinade and vegetables in medium saucepan. Bring to a boil; cook, stirring, until vegetables are tender.

Serve chicken and vegetables sprinkled with parsley.

serves 4
per serving 25.3g fat; 1745kJ
on the table in 35 minutes

11

sesame beef and noodles

500g beef rump steak, sliced thinly
1 tablespoon peanut oil
1 teaspoon sesame oil
1 teaspoon bottled crushed garlic
375g dried rice noodles
300g broccoli
2 tablespoons sesame seeds
¼ cup (60ml) oyster sauce
¼ cup (60ml) sweet chilli sauce

Combine beef, oils and garlic in medium bowl.
Place noodles in large heatproof bowl, cover with boiling water; stand until just tender, drain.
Meanwhile, add broccoli to small saucepan of boiling water; drain.
Stir-fry beef mixture in heated wok or large frying pan, in batches, until beef is browned. Stir-fry seeds until they pop.
Return beef to wok with noodles, broccoli and sauces; stir-fry until hot.

serves 4
per serving 16.5g fat; 2414kJ
on the table in 25 minutes

honey chilli chicken

1 tablespoon peanut oil
1kg chicken
  tenderloins, sliced
2 teaspoons bottled
  chopped chilli
1 teaspoon bottled
  grated ginger
1 large red capsicum
  (350g), sliced thickly
1 teaspoon cornflour
1 tablespoon soy sauce
⅓ cup (80ml) lemon juice
¼ cup (90g) honey
4 green onions,
  chopped finely

Heat half of the oil in wok or large frying pan; stir-fry chicken, chilli and ginger, in batches, until chicken is browned. Heat remaining oil in wok; stir-fry capsicum until just tender.
Blend cornflour in small jug with sauce, stir in juice and honey.
Return chicken mixture to wok with honey mixture; cook, stirring, until mixture boils and thickens slightly. Serve sprinkled with onion.

serves 4
per serving 18.6g fat; 2022kJ
on the table in 25 minutes

chicken marsala

7 canned anchovy fillets,
drained, chopped finely
1 tablespoon drained
capers, chopped finely
1 teaspoon dried
parsley flakes
1 teaspoon bottled
crushed garlic
1 tablespoon olive oil
4 single chicken breast
fillets (700g)
125g mozzarella cheese
¼ cup (60ml) marsala
1 cup (250ml)
chicken stock
½ cup (125ml) cream

Combine anchovy, capers, parsley and garlic
in small bowl.

Heat oil in large frying pan; cook chicken until
browned both sides. Remove chicken from pan.

Cut cheese into four even slices. Spread anchovy
mixture evenly on top of chicken, top with cheese.

Return chicken to pan; cook, covered, about
10 minutes or until chicken is cooked through and
cheese is melted. Remove from pan; keep warm.

Add marsala and stock to same pan, bring to
a boil; simmer, uncovered, about 5 minutes or
until reduced by a third. Stir in cream; simmer,
uncovered, 5 minutes or until thickened slightly.
Spoon sauce over chicken to serve.

serves 4
per serving 35.7g fat; 2426kJ
on the table in 40 minutes

balinese lamb chops

1 tablespoon peanut oil
12 lamb loin chops (1.2kg), trimmed
2 small brown onions (160g), sliced thinly
½ cup (130g) crunchy peanut butter
¼ cup (60ml) sweet chilli sauce
2 tablespoons lemon juice
⅔ cup (160ml) coconut milk
¾ cup (180ml) water
2 tablespoons coarsely chopped
    fresh coriander

Heat oil in large frying pan; cook lamb until browned and cooked as desired. Remove lamb from pan; drain excess fat from pan.
Add onion to pan; cook, stirring, until browned. Add peanut butter, sauce, juice, and combined coconut milk and water; cook, stirring, until sauce thickens slightly.
Return lamb to pan, coat with sauce. Serve sprinkled with coriander.

serves 4
per serving 45.9g fat; 2862kJ
on the table in 30 minutes

lamb cutlets with sweet citrus sauce

2 tablespoons olive oil
8 lamb cutlets (600g)

sweet citrus sauce
1 tablespoon grated
   orange rind
⅓ cup (80ml)
   orange juice
2 tablespoons
   lemon juice
½ cup (160g)
   redcurrant jelly
1 tablespoon
   red wine vinegar

Heat oil in large frying pan; cook lamb until
browned and cooked as desired.
Serve lamb with sweet citrus sauce; accompany
with mashed potatoes and rocket, if desired.
Sweet citrus sauce Combine rind, juices, jelly
and vinegar in medium saucepan; stir over heat
until jelly melts. Bring to a boil; reduce heat.
Simmer, uncovered, until sauce thickens slightly.

serves 4
per serving 16.1g fat; 1235kJ
on the table in 30 minutes

tandoori lamb with cucumber raita

1 tablespoon
tandoori paste
1⅓ cups (375g) yogurt
8 lamb fillets (640g)
1 lebanese cucumber
(130g), seeded,
chopped finely
2 green onions,
chopped finely
1 teaspoon ground
cardamom
½ teaspoon
ground cumin
2 cups (400g)
basmati rice
pinch saffron threads

Combine paste and half of the yogurt in medium
bowl; add lamb. Combine remaining yogurt in
small bowl with cucumber, onion and half of
the combined spices.

Place rice and saffron in large saucepan of
boiling water; cook, uncovered, until rice is tender.
Drain rice; place in large bowl. Toast remaining
spices in heated dry small frying pan until fragrant;
stir into saffron rice, cover to keep warm.

Cook undrained lamb, in batches, on heated
oiled grill plate (or grill or barbecue) until browned
and cooked as desired. Serve sliced lamb on
saffron rice, topped with cucumber raita.

serves 4
per serving 12.2g fat; 2723kJ
on the table in 30 minutes

tip You can use saffron powder instead of threads.

seafood salad

1 teaspoon olive oil
1 small brown onion
  (80g), sliced thinly
1 teaspoon bottled
  crushed garlic
500g packet frozen
  seafood marinara
  mix, thawed
375g large pasta shells
1 tablespoon dry
  white wine
½ cup (150g)
  mayonnaise
2 teaspoons
  worcestershire sauce
⅓ cup (80ml)
  tomato sauce
¼ teaspoon
  Tabasco sauce
1 tablespoon coarsely
  chopped fresh
  flat-leaf parsley
100g baby rocket leaves

Heat oil in large frying pan; cook onion and garlic,
stirring, until onion is soft. Add marinara mix; cook,
stirring, 5 minutes or until seafood is cooked through.
Place mixture in large bowl, cover; refrigerate.
Meanwhile, cook pasta in large saucepan of
boiling water, uncovered, until just tender; drain.
Rinse under cold water; drain.
Place pasta and combined wine, mayonnaise,
sauces and parsley in bowl with marinara mixture;
toss to combine. Serve seafood salad on rocket.

serves 4
per serving 18.1g fat; 2768kJ
on the table in 40 minutes

spaghetti marinara

1 tablespoon olive oil
1 medium brown onion
  (150g), chopped finely
⅓ cup (80ml) dry
  white wine
⅓ cup (95g)
  tomato paste
2 x 425g cans tomatoes
500g packet frozen
  seafood marinara
  mix, thawed
¼ cup coarsely chopped
  fresh flat-leaf parsley
375g spaghetti

Heat oil in large frying pan; cook onion, stirring, until soft. Add wine, paste and undrained crushed tomatoes to pan; bring to a boil. Reduce heat; simmer, uncovered, about 10 minutes or until sauce thickens slightly. Add marinara mix; cook, stirring occasionally, about 5 minutes or until seafood is cooked through. Stir in parsley.

Meanwhile, cook pasta in large saucepan of boiling water, uncovered, until just tender; drain.

Serve marinara mixture on top of pasta.

serves 4
per serving 9.8g fat; 2482kJ
on the table in 25 minutes

fish with antipasto salad

2 tablespoons olive oil
4 white fish cutlets (800g)
2 x 280g jars antipasto
    vegetables, drained
½ cup fresh flat-leaf parsley
1 large red onion (300g),
    sliced thinly
2 tablespoons lemon juice

Heat oil in large frying pan, add fish; cook until browned on both sides and cooked through.
Meanwhile, combine antipasto vegetables with parsley, onion and juice in medium bowl.
Serve fish with antipasto mixture.

serves 4
per serving 30.5g fat; 2206kJ
on the table in 15 minutes

tuna with shells, capers, olives and green beans

375g small pasta shells
2 cups (220g) frozen
   chopped green beans
2 x 125g cans smoked
   tuna slices in
   vegetable oil, drained
150g seeded black
   olives, halved
1 medium red capsicum
   (200g), sliced thinly
¼ cup (60ml) olive oil
¼ cup (60ml) white
   wine vinegar
2 tablespoons drained
   capers, chopped
1 teaspoon bottled
   crushed garlic

Cook pasta in large saucepan of boiling
water, uncovered, until just tender; drain.
Rinse under cold water; drain.
Meanwhile, boil, steam or microwave beans
until just tender; rinse under cold water; drain.
Place pasta and beans in large bowl with tuna,
olives, capsicum and combined remaining
ingredients; toss gently to combine.

serves 4
per serving 22.3g fat; 2557kJ
on the table in 30 minutes

fish with spiced beetroot

1 tablespoon olive oil
4 blue-eye cutlets (1kg)
425g can beetroot
  wedges, drained
1 teaspoon ground cumin
1 teaspoon ground
  coriander
1 teaspoon bottled
  crushed garlic
½ cup (140g) yogurt

Heat oil in large frying pan; cook fish until brown on both sides and cooked through.
Meanwhile, combine beetroot, spices and garlic in small bowl.
Serve fish topped with beetroot mixture and yogurt, and mixed salad leaves, if desired.

serves 4
per serving 11.1g fat; 1408kJ
on the table in 15 minutes

steak with mustard peppercorn sauce

50g butter
1 tablespoon olive oil
4 boneless beef sirloin
  steaks (800g)
1 teaspoon bottled
  crushed garlic
1 tablespoon
  seeded mustard
2 teaspoons canned,
  drained green
  peppercorns
1 cup (250ml) dry
  white wine
1 tablespoon finely
  chopped fresh basil
40g butter, extra

Heat butter and oil in large frying pan, add beef; cook until brown and cooked as desired, remove from pan.

Add garlic, mustard, peppercorns, wine and basil to same pan; stir over heat 2 minutes. Remove pan from heat; quickly stir through extra butter.

Serve beef with mustard peppercorn sauce; accompany with grilled flat mushrooms and mashed potato, if desired.

serves 4
per serving 35.5g fat; 2199kJ
on the table in 20 minutes

steak with honey and mustard glaze

2 teaspoons olive oil
4 boneless beef sirloin
    steaks (800g)
2 tablespoons honey
⅓ cup (80ml) lemon juice
½ teaspoon dried
    thyme leaves
1 tablespoon
    seeded mustard
1 teaspoon bottled
    crushed garlic

Heat oil in large frying pan, add beef; cook until
brown and cooked as desired, remove from pan.
Add remaining ingredients to same pan, bring
to a boil; reduce heat. Simmer, uncovered, until
mixture thickens slightly. Serve glaze over steaks.

serves 4
per serving 14.9g fat; 1459kJ
on the table in 20 minutes

smoked fish kedgeree

1 cup (200g) long-grain white rice
400g packet frozen smoked
    cod fish steaks, thawed
60g butter
⅓ cup coarsely chopped fresh flat-leaf parsley
1 tablespoon lemon juice
2 hard-boiled eggs, peeled, chopped

Cook rice in large saucepan of boiling water until tender; drain.
Meanwhile, poach fish in large frying pan of shallow boiling water until tender; drain, flake fish.
Melt butter in large saucepan, stir in rice, parsley and juice. Gently stir in fish and egg; cook over low heat until heated through.

serves 2
per serving 32.8g fat; 3442kJ
on the table in 25 minutes

steak with white bean salad

1 tablespoon olive oil
4 beef minute
   steaks (400g)
40g butter
½ teaspoon bottled
   crushed garlic
⅓ cup (80ml) beef stock

white bean salad
2 x 300g cans butter
   beans, rinsed, drained
2 large tomatoes (500g),
   chopped coarsely
2 trimmed sticks celery
   (150g), sliced thinly
2 tablespoons chopped
   fresh chives
¼ cup fresh basil
   leaves, torn
¼ cup (60ml) olive oil
¼ cup (60ml)
   lemon juice
1 teaspoon bottled
   crushed garlic

Heat oil in large frying pan, add beef; cook until
brown on both sides and cooked as desired.
Remove beef from pan; cover to keep warm.
Add butter and garlic to same pan, then stir
in stock. Bring to a boil; simmer, uncovered,
until reduced slightly. Serve beef with sauce
and white bean salad.
White bean salad Combine beans, tomato,
celery and herbs in medium bowl. Add
combined remaining ingredients; toss gently.

serves 4
per serving 31.4g fat; 1710kJ
on the table in 20 minutes

750g beef rump steak,
sliced thinly

35g packet taco
seasoning

2 tablespoons peanut oil

1 large red onion (300g),
sliced thinly

1 medium red capsicum
(200g), sliced thinly

1 medium yellow
capsicum (200g),
sliced thinly

4 small tomatoes (520g),
chopped coarsely

¼ cup coarsely chopped
fresh coriander

Combine beef and seasoning in large bowl. Heat
half of the oil in wok or large frying pan; stir-fry
beef and onion, in batches, until well browned.
Heat remaining oil in wok; stir-fry capsicums
until just tender. Combine beef mixture, capsicum
and remaining ingredients in large bowl.
Serve with flour tortillas, if desired.

serves 4
per serving 18.5g fat; 1689kJ
on the table in 25 minutes

cantonese-style beef

750g piece beef fillet
2 teaspoons sugar
2 teaspoons cornflour
1 tablespoon soy sauce
1 tablespoon oyster sauce
2 tablespoons dry sherry
2 medium brown
  onions (300g)
1 tablespoon peanut oil
2 cups (160g)
  bean sprouts

Trim fat and sinew from beef. Cut beef into 5mm-thick slices, flatten slightly with a meat mallet. Combine beef in medium bowl with sugar, cornflour, sauces and half of the sherry.
Cut onions into thin wedges. Heat half of the oil in wok or large frying pan; stir-fry onion until just tender, remove from wok. Heat remaining oil in wok; stir-fry beef, in batches, until browned.
Return beef to wok with remaining sherry, onion and sprouts; stir-fry until combined.

serves 4
per serving 13.7g fat; 1438kJ
on the table in 30 minutes

1 tablespoon peanut oil
1 teaspoon sesame oil
600g piece beef rump
    steak, sliced thinly
1 medium brown onion
    (150g), sliced
1 teaspoon bottled
    crushed garlic
230g can bamboo
    shoots, drained
½ cup (40g) bean sprouts
¼ cup (60ml)
    teriyaki sauce
⅓ cup (80ml) beef stock
450g hokkien noodles
4 green onions, sliced

Heat oils in wok or large frying pan; stir-fry beef, in batches, until browned.

Add onion, garlic and bamboo shoots to wok; stir-fry 2 minutes. Return beef to wok with sprouts. Stir in sauce and stock; stir-fry until mixture boils.

Rinse noodles under hot water; drain. Transfer noodles to large bowl; separate with fork.

Serve teriyaki beef stir-fry with noodles; sprinkle with green onion.

serves 4
per serving 13.1g fat; 1695kJ
on the table in 35 minutes

veal campagnola

4 large veal steaks (500g)
¼ cup (35g) plain flour
30g butter
2 cups (500ml) bottled tomato
    pasta sauce
3 cups (200g) thawed, drained
    loose leaf frozen spinach
2 cups (200g) grated mozzarella cheese

Place veal between pieces of plastic
wrap; pound until each veal piece
is of the same thickness. Discard
plastic wrap. Toss veal in flour;
shake away excess flour.
Heat butter in large frying pan, add
veal; cook until browned both sides,
drain on absorbent paper.
Add pasta sauce to same pan, bring
to a boil; place veal, in a single layer,
on top of boiling sauce. Spread quarter
of the spinach on top of each piece
of veal, then top with cheese. Cover;
let mixture simmer about 1 minute
or until cheese melts.

serves 4
per serving 21.5g fat; 1881kJ
on the table in 20 minutes

tunisian-style beef

500g beef rump steak, sliced thinly
1 teaspoon bottled crushed garlic
1 teaspoon bottled grated ginger
¼ cup (60ml) orange juice
1 tablespoon white wine vinegar
2 teaspoons ground coriander
1 teaspoon mixed spice
½ cup (100g) couscous
½ cup (125ml) boiling water
20g butter
2 tablespoons olive oil
1 medium red onion (170g), chopped finely
4 medium tomatoes (760g), chopped finely
¼ cup finely chopped fresh mint
¼ cup finely chopped fresh flat-leaf parsley
2 tablespoons lemon juice

Combine beef, garlic, ginger, orange juice, vinegar, coriander and mixed spice in large bowl.

Combine couscous, the boiling water and butter in medium heatproof bowl, cover; stand 5 minutes or until water is absorbed, fluffing with fork occasionally.

Heat half of the oil in wok or large frying pan; stir-fry beef mixture and onion, in batches, until beef is browned. Heat remaining oil in wok; stir-fry tomato until hot.

Return beef mixture to wok with couscous, herbs and lemon juice; stir-fry, tossing to combine.

serves 4
per serving 19.6g fat; 1773kJ
on the table in 40 minutes

veal parmesan

1 tablespoon olive oil
4 large veal
  steaks (500g)
1 cup (250ml) bottled
  tomato pasta sauce
1 cup (100g) grated
  mozzarella cheese
½ cup (40g) grated
  parmesan cheese

Heat oil in large frying pan; cook veal until browned lightly and cooked as desired. Transfer veal to shallow flameproof dish.
Add sauce to same reheated frying pan; cook until heated through. Spoon sauce over veal, top with cheeses; grill until cheese melts and is browned.
Serve with steamed asparagus and roasted potatoes and onions, if desired.

serves 4
per serving 16.8g fat; 1377kJ
on the table in 35 minutes

veal with capers and parsley

2 tablespoons olive oil
8 veal steaks (800g)
1 teaspoon bottled
  crushed garlic
½ cup (125ml) dry
  white wine
½ cup (125ml)
  beef stock
2 tablespoons coarsely
  chopped fresh
  flat-leaf parsley
¼ cup (50g) drained,
  coarsely chopped
  capers

Heat oil in large frying pan; cook veal over high heat, in batches, until browned both sides and cooked as desired. Remove from pan; cover to keep warm.

Add garlic to pan; stir until fragrant. Add wine and stock to pan; bring to a boil. Reduce heat; simmer, uncovered, 2 minutes. Stir in parsley and capers.

Serve sliced veal with sauce; accompany with mashed potatoes, if desired.

serves 4
per serving 14g fat; 1371kJ
on the table in 20 minutes

veal cutlets with tomato basil sauce

1 tablespoon olive oil
4 veal cutlets (600g)
2 x 425g cans tomatoes
½ cup (125ml) water
1 teaspoon bottled
  chopped red chilli
1 teaspoon bottled
  crushed garlic
2 teaspoons sugar
2 tablespoons
  balsamic vinegar
2 tablespoons torn
  fresh basil leaves

Heat oil in large frying pan; cook veal until
browned both sides and cooked as desired.
Remove veal from pan; keep warm.
Add undrained crushed tomatoes, the water, chilli,
garlic and sugar to pan; bring to a boil. Reduce
heat; simmer, uncovered, about 15 minutes or
until sauce has thickened. Stir in vinegar and
basil; cook, stirring, 2 minutes.
Serve veal with tomato basil sauce; accompany
with steamed potatoes and baby beans, if desired.

serves 4
per serving 7.9g fat; 926kJ
on the table in 40 minutes

pork with maple mustard sauce

4 pork midloin butterfly steaks (800g)
2 tablespoons seeded mustard
¼ cup (60ml) maple syrup
1 tablespoon finely chopped
  fresh flat-leaf parsley
1 tablespoon olive oil
½ cup (125ml) dry white wine

Place pork in shallow dish, pour over combined mustard, syrup and parsley; stand 10 minutes. Drain pork, reserving marinade.
Heat oil in large frying pan, add pork; cook until browned both sides and cooked through. Remove pork from pan; cover to keep warm.
Combine reserved marinade and wine in same pan, bring to a boil; simmer, uncovered, until thickened slightly. Serve sauce over pork, with steamed snow peas, if desired.

serves 4
per serving 11.8g fat; 1501kJ
on the table in 35 minutes

peppered veal medallions

8 veal medallions (640g)
2 tablespoons drained,
  canned green
  peppercorns,
  chopped finely
½ cup (125ml) brandy
1 tablespoon olive oil
1 cup (250ml) water
2 teaspoons cornflour
⅓ cup (80g) sour cream

Combine veal, peppercorns and brandy in medium bowl, cover; stand 10 minutes.
Drain veal; reserve marinade. Heat oil in large frying pan; cook veal until browned both sides and cooked as desired. Remove from pan; keep warm.
Combine reserved marinade and blended water and cornflour in same pan; bring to a boil. Remove from heat; stir in cream. Simmer about 5 minutes or until thickened. Serve sauce poured over veal; accompany with steamed beans, if desired.

serves 4
per serving 16.3g fat; 1516kJ
on the table in 40 minutes

pork and noodle stir-fry

⅓ cup (80ml)
    barbecue sauce
2 tablespoons
    plum sauce
2 tablespoons
    hoisin sauce
2 tablespoons peanut oil
1 teaspoon bottled
    crushed garlic
750g pork fillet,
    sliced thinly
450g hokkien noodles
2 corn cobs (800g),
    sliced thickly
1 medium white onion
    (150g), sliced thinly
1 large red capsicum
    (350g), chopped
    coarsely
150g snow peas
1 cup (80g) bean sprouts

Combine sauces, half of the oil and garlic in large jug. Place pork in large bowl, pour half of the sauce mixture over pork.

Rinse noodles under hot water; drain. Transfer to large bowl; separate noodles with fork. Boil, steam or microwave corn until tender; drain.

Meanwhile, heat remaining oil in wok or large frying pan; stir-fry pork mixture, in batches, until browned. Add onion and capsicum; stir-fry until just tender.

Return pork to wok with noodles, corn, snow peas, sprouts and remaining sauce; cook, stirring, until hot.

serves 4
per serving 16.5g fat; 2893kJ
on the table in 30 minutes

deli pasta salad

500g large spiral pasta
150g bottled char-grilled
    eggplant, drained,
    chopped coarsely
150g bottled char-grilled
    capsicum, drained,
    chopped coarsely
1 cup (150g) drained
    sun-dried tomatoes
150g sliced salami,
    cut into strips
⅓ cup small fresh
    basil leaves

pesto dressing
1 cup (250ml) bottled
    italian dressing
2 tablespoons basil pesto

Cook pasta in large saucepan of boiling water,
uncovered, until just tender. Drain pasta, rinse
under cold water.
Combine pasta with remaining ingredients and
pesto dressing in large bowl.
Pesto dressing Combine dressing and pesto.

serves 6
per serving 36.3g fat; 3054kJ
on the table in 20 minutes

chickpea and pumpkin curry

2 teaspoons peanut oil
2 medium brown onions
  (300g), sliced thinly
1 teaspoon bottled
  crushed garlic
2 tablespoons tikka
  curry paste
3 cups (750ml)
  vegetable stock
1kg butternut pumpkin,
  chopped coarsely
300g can chickpeas,
  rinsed, drained
1 cup (125g) frozen peas
¼ cup (60ml) cream
2 tablespoons finely
  chopped fresh
  coriander

Heat oil in large saucepan; cook onion and garlic, stirring, until onion is soft. Add paste; cook, stirring, until fragrant.
Stir in stock, bring to a boil; add pumpkin. Reduce heat; simmer, covered, 15 minutes or until pumpkin is almost tender.
Add chickpeas and peas to curry; cook, stirring, until hot. Stir in cream and coriander.

serves 4
per serving 15.1g fat; 1277kJ
on the table in 35 minutes

moroccan cutlets with couscous

12 lamb cutlets (900g), trimmed
45g jar moroccan seasoning
2 cups (400g) couscous
2 cups (500ml) boiling water
8 dried dates, sliced thinly
½ cup (80g) pine nuts, toasted
2 tablespoons coarsely chopped
  fresh coriander

Coat lamb in seasoning. Cook lamb on heated oiled grill plate (or grill or barbecue) until browned both sides and cooked as desired.
Meanwhile, place couscous in large heatproof bowl, cover with the water; stand, covered, 5 minutes. Fluff couscous with fork. Stir in dates, pine nuts and coriander.
Serve lamb with couscous mixture.

serves 4
per serving 25.5g fat; 3154kJ
on the table in 25 minutes

lentil vegetable soup

1 tablespoon olive oil
1 teaspoon bottled
  crushed garlic
1 medium brown onion
  (150g), chopped finely
2 medium carrots (240g),
  chopped finely
2 trimmed sticks celery
  (150g), chopped finely
1 cup (200g) red lentils
3 cups (750ml) water
3 cups (750ml)
  chicken stock
1 bay leaf
425g can tomatoes
1 tablespoon tomato paste
2 tablespoons finely
  chopped fresh
  flat-leaf parsley

Heat oil in large saucepan; cook garlic,
onion, carrot and celery until onion is soft.
Stir in lentils, the water, stock, bay leaf,
undrained crushed tomatoes and paste.
Bring to a boil; simmer, covered, about
20 minutes or until lentils are soft. Discard
bay leaf. Serve sprinkled with parsley.

serves 4
per serving 6.7g fat; 1016kJ
on the table in 45 minutes

chicken, corn and noodle chowder

1 teaspoon peanut oil
1 medium brown
  onion (150g),
  chopped coarsely
1 teaspoon bottled
  crushed garlic
420g can corn
  kernels, drained
750g can small potatoes,
  drained, quartered
1 litre (4 cups)
  chicken stock
375g chicken
  tenderloins, chopped
150g dried egg noodles
2 tablespoons sour cream
1 tablespoon finely
  shredded fresh
  flat-leaf parsley

Heat oil in large saucepan; cook onion
and garlic, stirring, until onion is soft.
Add corn, potato and stock; bring to
a boil. Reduce heat; simmer, covered,
10 minutes. Blend or process potato
mixture, in batches, until smooth.
Return potato mixture to same pan,
add chicken and noodles; simmer,
uncovered, about 10 minutes or until
chicken is cooked through.
Serve topped with sour cream
and parsley.

serves 4
per serving 12.6g fat; 2022kJ
on the table in 35 minutes

sweet corn soup

1 tablespoon olive oil
1 medium white onion
  (150g), chopped
1 teaspoon bottled
  crushed garlic
1 litre (4 cups)
  chicken stock
2 cups (320g) frozen
  corn kernels
130g can creamed corn
1 medium potato (200g),
  chopped coarsely
¼ cup (60ml) cream
50g plain corn chips
1 tablespoon coarsely
  chopped fresh chives

Heat oil in large saucepan, add onion and garlic;
cook, stirring, until onion is soft.
Add stock, 1 cup of the corn kernels, creamed corn
and potato; bring to a boil. Reduce heat; simmer,
uncovered, about 15 minutes or until potato is tender.
Blend or process soup, in batches, until smooth.
Return soup to pan; stir in remaining corn kernels
and cream. Stir over low heat until corn is tender.
Serve soup with crumbled corn chips and chives.

serves 4
per serving 16.9g fat; 1420kJ
on the table in 45 minutes

pea and potato soup

3 cups (750ml)
chicken stock
2 medium leeks (700g),
sliced thinly
1 teaspoon bottled
crushed garlic
2 medium potatoes (400g),
chopped coarsely
4 cups (500g) frozen peas
3 cups (750ml) water
2 tablespoons finely
shredded fresh mint

Heat 2 tablespoons of the stock in large
saucepan, add leek and garlic; cook, stirring,
about 10 minutes or until leek is soft.
Add remaining stock, potato, peas and the water;
bring to a boil. Reduce heat; simmer, covered,
about 15 minutes or until vegetables are tender.
Blend or process soup, in batches, until smooth.
Return soup to same cleaned pan; stir over heat
until hot. Serve sprinkled with mint.

serves 4
per serving 1.9g fat; 781kJ
on the table in 40 minutes

chilli beans with spicy tortilla crisps

1 tablespoon olive oil
2 medium brown onions
   (300g), chopped finely
1 teaspoon bottled
   crushed garlic
1 medium red capsicum
   (200g), chopped finely
420g can red kidney
   beans, rinsed, drained
400g can borlotti beans,
   rinsed, drained
2 x 425g cans tomatoes
2 teaspoons bottled
   chopped red chilli
½ cup (125ml)
   vegetable stock
1 tablespoon
   tomato paste
2 tablespoons
   finely chopped
   fresh coriander
2 x 18cm flour tortillas
cooking-oil spray
½ teaspoon mexican
   chilli powder
½ medium avocado
   (125g), chopped finely

Preheat oven to very hot.
Heat oil in large frying pan; cook onion and
garlic until onion is soft. Add capsicum, beans,
undrained crushed tomatoes, chilli, stock and
paste; simmer, uncovered, about 30 minutes
or until thickened. Stir in coriander.
Meanwhile, cut tortillas into wedges; place on
oven trays. Spray with cooking-oil spray, sprinkle
with chilli powder; bake, uncovered, in very hot
oven about 8 minutes or until browned and crisp.
Serve chilli beans with tortilla crisps and avocado.

serves 4
per serving 13.1g fat; 1617kJ
on the table in 45 minutes

chicken and tomato omelette

½ cup (125ml)
  chicken stock
⅓ cup (20g) dehydrated
  sun-dried tomatoes
170g chicken breast
  fillet, chopped finely
1 medium brown onion
  (150g), chopped finely
1 teaspoon bottled
  crushed garlic
2 eggs, beaten lightly
4 egg whites,
  beaten lightly
1 tablespoon finely
  chopped fresh chives

Bring stock to a boil in small saucepan, add tomatoes; simmer, uncovered, about 5 minutes or until tomatoes soften. Drain tomatoes, reserving 1 tablespoon of the stock; chop tomatoes.

Combine chicken, reserved stock, onion and garlic in an 18cm oiled non-stick frying pan; cook, stirring, until chicken is browned.

Meanwhile, combine tomato, egg, egg white and chives in medium bowl.

Pour over chicken mixture; cook over low heat about 5 minutes or until egg mixture is almost set, tilting pan occasionally. Place pan under heated grill until omelette is set and lightly browned on top.

serves 2
per serving 10.8g fat; 1151kJ
on the table in 30 minutes

honey-mustard chicken with potato-kumara mash

8 chicken tenderloins (600g)
⅓ cup (115g) honey
2 tablespoons seeded mustard
⅓ cup (80ml) white vinegar
2 tablespoons soy sauce
3 medium potatoes (600g), chopped coarsely
1 small kumara (250g), chopped coarsely
1 teaspoon bottled crushed garlic
¼ cup (60ml) milk

Preheat oven to hot. Thread chicken onto eight bamboo skewers; place in shallow baking dish.
Pour half of the combined honey, mustard, vinegar and sauce over chicken. Cook chicken, uncovered, in hot oven about 15 minutes or until cooked through.
Meanwhile, boil, steam or microwave combined potato and kumara until tender; drain. Mash in medium bowl with garlic and milk.
Heat remaining marinade in small saucepan. Serve chicken with potato-kumara mash; drizzle with marinade.

serves 4
per serving 9.2g fat; 1814kJ
on the table in 35 minutes

tip Soak bamboo skewers in water for an hour before use to prevent them from splintering and/or scorching. You can grill or barbecue the chicken rather than bake it.

pasta with pizzaiola sauce

1 tablespoon olive oil
2 x 425g cans tomatoes
1 teaspoon bottled
  crushed garlic
1 tablespoon finely
  chopped fresh oregano
2 tablespoons finely
  chopped fresh
  flat-leaf parsley
250g spaghetti

Heat oil in large frying pan, add undrained crushed tomatoes and garlic; bring to a boil. Reduce heat; simmer, uncovered, about 30 minutes or until reduced by half. Stir in herbs.
Meanwhile, cook pasta in large saucepan of boiling water until tender; drain. Combine with sauce to serve.

serves 2
per serving 11.5g fat; 2531kJ
on the table in 40 minutes

spaghetti with tomato and white beans

⅓ cup (80ml)
  vegetable stock
1 small red onion
  (100g), chopped finely
1 teaspoon bottled
  crushed garlic
1 cup (250ml) dry
  white wine
½ teaspoon sugar
2 cups (500ml) bottled
  tomato pasta sauce
375g spaghetti
1 tablespoon coarsely
  chopped fresh oregano
2 tablespoons
  drained capers,
  chopped coarsely
½ cup (60g) seeded
  black olives, quartered
300g can butter beans,
  rinsed, drained
2 tablespoons coarsely
  chopped fresh
  flat-leaf parsley

Heat half of the stock in medium saucepan;
cook onion and garlic, stirring, until onion is soft.
Stir in wine, remaining stock, sugar and sauce;
bring to a boil. Reduce heat; simmer, uncovered,
until sauce thickens slightly.
Meanwhile, cook pasta in large saucepan of
boiling water, uncovered, until just tender; drain.
Stir remaining ingredients into sauce; cook,
stirring, until hot. Serve spaghetti with tomato
and white beans.

serves 4
per serving 2.4g fat; 1940kJ
on the table in 30 minutes

desserts from the shelf

1

Coarsely crush chocolate-coated coffee beans in a food processor; stir through softened vanilla ice-cream.

2

For an instant trifle, dip savoiardi sponge fingers into cranberry juice, arrange in serving glasses; top with yogurt and fresh berries.

3

Dip strawberries into melted white, dark or milk chocolate for a sweet treat.

4

Cut down both sides of a mango to remove cheeks. Score mango flesh at 1.5cm intervals, then score in opposite direction. Sprinkle mango flesh with brown sugar; grill 5 minutes or until lightly browned. Serve squeezed with fresh lime juice.

5

Heat a little butter in a medium frying pan. Add peeled, cored and sliced apple; sprinkle with brown sugar, ground cinnamon and a little cream. Cook, stirring, until apples are just tender. Serve over toasted raisin bread.

6

Combine ⅓ cup honey and ½ cup lime juice in small saucepan, bring to a boil; simmer, uncovered, 5 minutes. Pour honey mixture over fresh fruit salad, serve with honey-flavoured yogurt.

7

Chop 180g Snickers chocolate bar, combine with ½ cup cream in small saucepan; stir over low heat (or microwave) until melted. Serve over hot toasted waffles and ice-cream.

8

Combine ⅔ cup lemon-flavoured spread with ⅓ cup cream in small saucepan; stir over low heat until smooth. Serve hot lemon sauce over ice-cream.

9

For a quick mango and passionfruit fool, combine mango puree and passionfruit pulp in medium bowl; swirl mixture through vanilla yogurt.

glossary

bamboo shoots creamy-yellow shoots of bamboo plants; available in cans.

bean sprouts also known as bean shoots.

beetroot also known as red beets or, simply, beets; firm, round root vegetable.

black bean sauce made from fermented soy beans, spices, water and flour.

borlotti beans also known as roman beans; pale-pink pod with dark-pink spots.

butter use salted or unsalted (sweet) butter; 125g is equal to one stick of butter.

butter beans cans labelled butter beans contain, in fact, cannellini beans. Butter beans is also another name for lima beans.

capers the grey-green buds of a shrub; sold either dried and salted, or pickled.

capsicum also known as bell pepper or, simply, pepper. Discard seeds and membranes before use.

cheese

cream: soft milk cheese that is commonly known as "Philly" or "Philadelphia".

mozzarella: a soft, spun-curd cheese; has a low melting point and wonderfully elastic texture when heated.

parmesan: also known as parmigiano; a hard, grainy cow-milk cheese.

chickpeas also called garbanzos, hummus or channa; irregularly round, sandy-coloured legume; available dried or canned.

coconut milk unsweetened, pure coconut milk in cans.

corn kernels sometimes called niblets; available in cans or frozen.

cornflour also known as cornstarch; used as a thickening agent in cooking.

couscous a fine, grain-like cereal product made from semolina.

creamed corn available in cans from supermarkets.

five-spice powder a fragrant mixture of ground cinnamon, cloves, star anise, sichuan pepper and fennel seeds.

flour, plain an all-purpose flour, made from wheat.

green peppercorns sold canned or bottled in brine.

hoisin sauce thick, sweet, spicy Chinese sauce made from salted fermented soy beans, onions and garlic.

kumara orange-fleshed sweet potato often confused with yam.

lebanese cucumber long, slender and thin-skinned; also known as the European or burpless cucumber.

maple syrup distilled sap of the maple tree; maple-flavoured syrup is not an adequate substitute.

marsala sweet fortified wine, originally from Sicily.

mexican chilli powder a blend of chilli powder, paprika, oregano, cumin, pepper and garlic.

mixed spice a blend of ground spices usually consisting of cinnamon, allspice and nutmeg.

mustard

french: plain mild mustard.

seeded: also known as wholegrain. A French-style coarse-grain mustard made from crushed mustard seeds and dijon-style French mustard.

noodles

dried egg: made from wheat flour and eggs; strands vary in thickness.

dried rice: made from rice flour and water, available flat and wide or very thin (vermicelli).

hokkien: also known as stir-fry noodles; fresh wheat-flour noodles resembling thick, yellow-brown spaghetti. Must be rinsed under hot water to remove starch and excess oil before use.

instant noodles: quick-cook noodles also known as 2-minute noodles; sold with a flavour sachet.

oil

peanut: pressed from ground peanuts; most commonly used oil in Asian cooking because of its high smoke point.

sesame: made from roasted, crushed white sesame seeds; used for flavour, not as a cooking medium.

onion

green: also known as scallion or (incorrectly) shallot; an immature onion picked before the bulb has formed, having a long, bright-green edible stalk.

red: also known as spanish, red spanish or bermuda onion; a sweet-flavoured, large, purple-red onion.

oyster sauce rich, brown sauce made from oysters and their brine, cooked with salt and soy sauce, and thickened with starches.

plum sauce a thick, sweet and sour dipping sauce made from plums, vinegar, sugar, chillies and spices.

pumpkin also known as squash; various types can be substituted for each other.

red kidney beans medium-sized red bean, slightly floury yet sweet in flavour.

rice, basmati a fragrant, long-grain white rice.

rocket also known as arugula, rugula and rucola; peppery-tasting green leaf.

saffron available in strands or ground form; imparts a yellow-orange colour to food once infused. Should be stored in the freezer.

sambal oelek (also ulek or olek) a salty paste made from ground chillies.

seafood marinara mix a mixture of uncooked seafood available fresh and frozen.

snickers chocolate bar a nougat, peanut and caramel bar, coated in chocolate.

snow peas also called mange tout ("eat all').

stock we used packaged liquid stock.

sugar we used coarse, granulated table sugar, also known as crystal sugar, unless otherwise specified.

brown: an extremely soft, fine granulated sugar retaining molasses for its characteristic colour and flavour.

caster: also known as superfine or finely granulated table sugar.

sweet chilli sauce a mild, Thai-style sauce made from red chillies, sugar, garlic and vinegar.

tabasco sauce brand name of an extremely fiery sauce made from vinegar, hot red peppers and salt.

taco seasoning packaged seasoning mix to duplicate the Mexican sauce made from oregano, cumin, chillies and other spices.

tandoori paste a blend of hot, fragrant Indian spices.

teriyaki sauce commercially bottled sauce made from soy sauce, mirin, sugar, ginger and other spices.

tikka curry paste consists of lentil flour, garlic, ginger, oil, chilli, coriander, cumin, and other spices.

tomato paste triple-concentrated tomato puree used to flavour soups, stews, sauces and casseroles.

tomato sauce also known as ketchup or catsup; a flavoured condiment made from tomatoes, vinegar and spices.

tortilla, flour thin, round, unleavened Mexican bread, made from flour.

vinegar
balsamic: authentic only from the province of Modena, Italy; aged in antique wooden casks to give the exquisite pungent flavour.

worcestershire sauce a thin, dark-brown spicy sauce.

zucchini also known as courgette.

index

facts and figures

These conversions are approximate only, but the difference between an exact and the approximate conversion of various liquid and dry measures is minimal and will not affect your cooking results.

Measuring equipment

The difference between one country's measuring cups and another's is, at most, within a 2 or 3 teaspoon variance. (For the record, 1 Australian metric measuring cup holds approximately 250ml.) The most accurate way of measuring dry ingredients is to weigh them. For liquids, use a clear glass or plastic jug having metric markings.

Note: NZ, Canada, USA and UK all use 15ml tablespoons. Australian tablespoons measure 20ml.
All cup and spoon measurements are level.

How to measure

When using graduated measuring cups, shake dry ingredients loosely into the appropriate cup. Do not tap the cup on a bench or tightly pack the ingredients unless directed to do so. Level the top of measuring cups and measuring spoons with a knife. When measuring liquids, place a clear glass or plastic jug having metric markings on a flat surface to check accuracy at eye level.

Dry Measures

metric	imperial
15g	1/2oz
30g	1oz
60g	2oz
90g	3oz
125g	4oz (¼lb)
155g	5oz
185g	6oz
220g	7oz
250g	8oz (½lb)
280g	9oz
315g	10oz
345g	11oz
375g	12oz (¾lb)
410g	13oz
440g	14oz
470g	15oz
500g	16oz (1lb)
750g	24oz (1½lb)
1kg	32oz (2lb)

We use large eggs having an average weight of 60g.

Liquid Measures

metric	imperial
30 ml	1 fluid oz
60 ml	2 fluid oz
100 ml	3 fluid oz
125 ml	4 fluid oz
150 ml	5 fluid oz (¼ pint/1 gill)
190 ml	6 fluid oz
250 ml (1cup)	8 fluid oz
300 ml	10 fluid oz (½ pint)
500 ml	16 fluid oz
600 ml	20 fluid oz (1 pint)
1000 ml (1litre)	1¾ pints

Helpful Measures

metric	imperial
3mm	⅛in
6mm	¼in
1cm	½in
2cm	¾in
2.5cm	1in
6cm	2½in
8cm	3in
20cm	8in
23cm	9in
25cm	10in
30cm	12in (1ft)

Oven Temperatures

These oven temperatures are only a guide.
Always check the manufacturer's manual.

	°C (Celsius)	°F (Fahrenheit)	Gas Mark
Very slow	120	250	1
Slow	150	300	2
Moderately slow	160	325	3
Moderate	180 –190	350 – 375	4
Moderately hot	200 – 210	400 – 425	5
Hot	220 – 230	450 – 475	6
Very hot	240 – 250	500 – 525	7

at your fingertips

These elegant slipcovers store up to 10 mini books and make the books instantly accessible.

And the metric measuring cups and spoons make following our recipes a piece of cake.

Book Holder
Australia: $13.10 (incl. GST).
Elsewhere: $A21.95.

Metric Measuring Set
Australia: $6.50 (incl. GST).
New Zealand: $A8.00.
Elsewhere: $A9.95.
Prices include postage and handling. This offer is available in all countries.

Photocopy and complete coupon below

Mail or fax Photocopy and complete the coupon below and post to
ACP Books Reader Offer,
ACP Publishing, GPO Box 4967,
Sydney NSW 2001, *or* fax to (02) 9267 4967.

Phone Have your credit card details ready, then phone 136 116 (Mon-Fri, 8.00am-6.00pm; Sat, 8.00am-6.00pm).

Australian residents
We accept the credit cards listed on the coupon, money orders and cheques.
Overseas residents We accept the credit cards listed on the coupon, drafts in $A drawn on an Australian bank, and also British, New Zealand and U.S. cheques in the currency of the country of issue. Credit card charges are at the exchange rate current at the time of payment.

☐ **Book Holder**   ☐ **Metric Measuring Set**
Please indicate number(s) required.

Mr/Mrs/Ms _____

Address _____

_____

Postcode _____ Country _____

Ph: Business hours ( ) _____

I enclose my cheque/money order for $ _____ payable to ACP Publishing.

OR: please charge $ _____ to my   ☐ Bankcard   ☐ Mastercard

☐ Visa   ☐ American Express   ☐ Diners Club

Expiry date ____ /____

Card number

Cardholder's signature _____

Please allow up to 30 days delivery within Australia.
Allow up to 6 weeks for overseas deliveries.
Both offers expire 31/12/03. HLMFTS02

Food director Pamela Clark
Food editor Louise Patniotis
ACP BOOKS STAFF
Editorial director Susan Tomnay
Creative director Hieu Nguyen
Senior editor Julie Collard
Designer Mary Keep
Publishing manager (sales) Jennifer McDon
Publishing manager (rights & new titles) Jane Hazell
Assistant brand manager Donna Gianniotis
Pre-press by Harry Palmer
Production manager Carol Currie
Publisher Sue Wannan
Group publisher Jill Baker
Chief executive officer John Alexander
Produced by ACP Books, Sydney.
Printing by Dai Nippon Printing in Hong Kon
Published by ACP Publishing Pty Limited,
54 Park St, Sydney; GPO Box 4088, Sydney,
NSW 1028. Ph: (02) 9282 8618
Fax: (02) 9267 9438.
acpbooks@acp.com.au
www.acpbooks.com.au
To order books phone 136 116.
Send recipe enquiries to
Recipeenquiries@acp.com.au
Australia Distributed by Network Services,
GPO Box 4088, Sydney, NSW 1028.
Ph: (02) 9282 8777 Fax: (02) 9264 3278.
United Kingdom Distributed by Australian
Consolidated Press (UK), Moulton Park Busin
Centre, Red House Road, Moulton Park,
Northampton, NN3 6AQ. Ph: (01604) 497 53
Fax: (01604) 497 533 acpukltd@aol.com
Canada Distributed by Whitecap Books Ltd,
351 Lynn Ave, North Vancouver, BC, V7J 2C
Ph: (604) 980 9852.
New Zealand Distributed by Netlink Distribu'
Company, Level 4, 23 Hargreaves St,
College Hill, Auckland 1, Ph: (9) 302 7616.
South Africa Distributed by: PSD Promotion
(Pty) Ltd, PO Box 1175, Isando 1600, SA,
Ph: (011) 392 6065.

Clark, Pamela.
From the shelf.

Includes index.
ISBN 1 86396 276 X

1. Quick and easy cookery.
I. Title: Australian Women's Weekly.
(Series: Australian Women's Weekly mini ser
641.555

© ACP Publishing Pty Limited 2002
ABN 18 053 273 546

Cover: Spaghetti with tomato and white beans, page 57.
Photographer Andre Martin
Stylist Sarah O'Brien
Home economist Amanda Kelly
Back cover: Lamb cutlets with sweet citrus sauce, page 18; Pork and noodle stir-fry, page 43.
Additional photography Stuart Scott
Additional styling Wendy Berecry
Home economist for additional photography Cathie Lonnie